COLOUR AND LEARN ABOUT GOD

GOD NEVER CHANGES

God never changes

A baby quickly changes and grows up to be a big child. But God never changes. "The boy Samuel grew up in the presence of the Lord."
1 Samuel 2:21

baby

— — — —

changes

— — — — — — —

child

— — — — —

Page 2 Key words:

baby

changes

child

God never changes

A bright sunny day changes into a dark night. But God never changes.
"He who turns blackness into dawn and darkens day into night - the
Lord is his name." Amos 5:8

sunny

— — — — —

God

— — —

night

— — — — —

Page 4 Key words:

sunny

God

night

Go over the words you have
learnt so far:

baby
changes
child
sunny
God
night

God never changes

Flowers in the garden change. They are bright and colourful for a time but then they wither. But God never changes. "As for man his days are like grass, he flourishes like a flower in the field; the wind blows over the flower, it is gone and then forgotten." Psalm 103:15-16.

flowers

— — — — — — —

wither

— — — — — —

gone

— — — —

Page 6 Key words:

flowers   wither   gone

Go over the words you have learnt so far:

baby   *wither*
changes   *gone*
child
sunny
God
night
flowers

God never changes

Our friends change. Some have to move away to other places. But God never changes. "There is a friend who sticks closer than a brother." Proverbs 18:24

friends

— — — — — — —

move

— — — —

brother

— — — — — — —

Page 8 Key words:

friends

move

brother

Go over the words you have learnt so far:

baby	flowers
changes	wither
child	gone
sunny	friends
God	move
night	brother

God never changes

Our moods change. Sometimes we are very sad. Sometimes we are happy. But God never changes. "You, God, remain the same and your years will never end." Pslam 102:27

sad

— — —

happy

— — — — —

same

— — — —

Page 10 Key words:

sad

happy

same

Go over the words you have learnt so far:

baby	flowers	sad
changes	wither	happy
child	gone	same
sunny	friends	
God	move	
night	brother	

God never changes

God never changes. He is the same yesterday and today and forever. "Jesus Christ is the same yesterday, today and forever." Hebrews 13:8

yesterday

— — — — — — — — —

today

— — — — —

forever

— — — — — — —

Page 12 Key words:

yesterday

today

forever

Go over the words you have learnt so far:

baby	flowers	sad
changes	wither	happy
child	gone	same
sunny	friends	yesterday
God	move	today
night	brother	forever

These are all the words that you have learnt in this book. Try and fit them into the gaps in the following story to see how well you have learnt them.

	God	friends	same
baby	night	move	yesterday
changes	flowers	brother	today
child	wither	sad	forever
sunny	gone	happy	

When you were a _ _ _ _ you were little. But a

baby _ _ _ _ _ _ _ and grows up into a big

_ _ _ _ _. Other things change. A wet day can

change into a _ _ _ _ _ day. But _ _ _ never

changes. Day time changes into _ _ _ _ _. But

God never changes. Colourful _ _ _ _ _ _ _

change. They _ _ _ _ _ _ and then they die

and are _ _ _ _. Sometimes people change.

Sometimes our __ __ __ __ __ __ __ change. They

__ __ __ __ to another town. But God never changes.

He will never leave you. He sticks closer to you than a

__ __ __ __ __ __ __. Sometimes you change. You

can be __ __ __ and then __ __ __ __ __. But God

never changes. God is the __ __ __ __. God is the

same __ __ __ __ __ __ __ __ __. God is the same

__ __ __ __ __. God is the same __ __ __ __ __ __ __ __.